# HONEY SHOWS

## Guidelines for exhibitors, superintendents, and judges

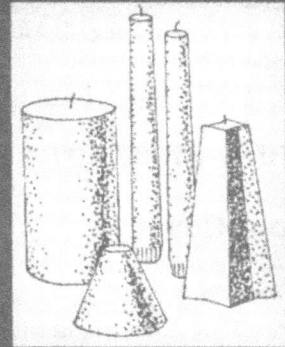

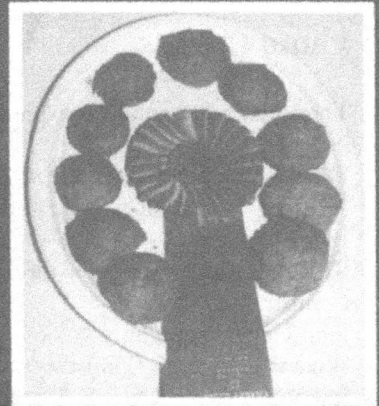

Roger A. and Mary Lou Morse

Copyright © 1996 Wicwas Press
P. O. Box 817
Cheshire, Connecticut 06410-0817
Phone/Fax 203-250-7575
E-Mail ljconnor@aol.com

## Library of Congress Cataloging-in-Publication Data

Morse, Roger A.
    Honey shows: guidelines for exhibitors, superintendents, and judges / by Roger A. and Mary Lou Morse.
    p. cm.
    Includes Index.
    1. Honey--Judging. 2. Honey--Exhibitions. I. Morse, Mary Lou. II. Title
TX560.H7M67 1996
638'.16'079--dc21              96-36939
                                  CIP

**ISBN 1-878075-07-1**

## Front Cover

Center—Peggy McCaig shows off the first prize for cut comb honey at the Eastern Apicultural Society annual Honey Show. Lower right and lower left—Chewy honey cookies and a bulk frame of honey (in traveling case) also received top class honors at EAS. Pen and ink drawings of mead and beeswax candles by David Heskes.

## Photo Credits

The authors and publisher express thanks to the photographers whose work appears in this publication. They include:

Eastern Apicultural Society *EAS Journal*—Featuring photos by Joe Hamel: Figures 5, 18, 19, 22, 23, 24, 26, 27, front cover cookies; —Featuring photos by Stephen McDaniel: Figures 1, 6, 17, front cover bulk honey, Peggy McCaig

Rick Fell: back cover honey through polariscope

Gamber Glass: 11

John Hogg: Figure 14

Wicwas Press, LLC (Dr. Lawrence J. Connor): Figures 12, 13, 15, 16, 17, 20, 25

Ray Williamson: Figure 2, 3, 4, 9, 10, 21, 29

All other photos were provided by the authors.

*A special thank you to all show entrants whose works are shown in these photos.*

*Figure 1. A honey show.*

# Table of Contents

Figure 2. Worker honey bee gathering nectar and pollen from a dandelion flower.

# Preface

A honey show is an opportunity for beekeepers to demonstrate their ability to package for show or market the same high-quality products that honey bees store in their hive. Many things can go wrong when honey and beeswax are removed from a colony and packaged for sale. For example, air may be added as the honey splashes against the side of an extractor, leaving a ring of foam around the inside top of a jar of liquid honey. Unsightly soot from a smoker may be blown onto the surface of a comb honey section. Honey may contain lint if it is strained through cheesecloth or a common cotton cloth. In the case of a comb of honey, bees may chew small holes in the cappings to feed on honey if they are smoked when the honey is removed. Beeswax may contain too much propolis or be dark for other reasons. These are just a few of the items that are discussed more fully in this text. A judge in a honey show searches for all the errors beekeepers can make when they prepare their products for sale.

Honey is one of the few natural, unrefined food products on the market today. Beekeepers are determined that the public continue to understand this, and they emphasize this fact at meetings, in writing, and at honey shows.

Only about 1.2 billion pounds of honey are produced worldwide in one year, less than one-fifth of a pound per person. Consumption in the United States is a little more than one pound per person, including honey used on the table and in bakeries. Honey is a luxury product, and only a small number of people in the world still enjoy honey stolen from natural nests in forests and caves.

Although the primary substances in honey are sugar and water, it also contains several other components ranging from pigments that give honeys their color to aromatic substances that give honeys their distinctive odors. Most honeys are light amber or golden in color, but one honey is blue, several have reddish or greenish tinges and some are jet black. The odors given by honeys also vary, some being far more striking than others. These variations must be considered when judging honey quality.

The beeswax produced by honey bees is no different from that produced by bees kept by the ancient Egyptians. There is no official grading system for beeswax, and the market is controlled by a small number of knowledgeable buyers. Because beeswax contains over 300 different compounds, it is a complex, variable substance that is difficult to judge.

A judge at a honey show expresses his or her opinion about the quality of the entries, taking into account all of the variations that may occur. However, the judge's opinion must be based on guidelines that both the judge and the exhibitor understand. We have written this book for the express purpose of making these guidelines clear.

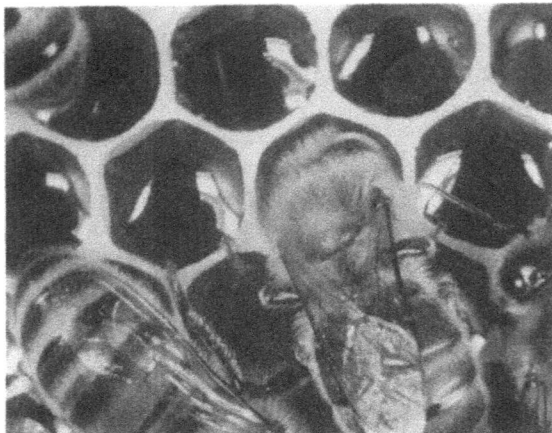

*Figure 3. Worker bees process nectar into honey and store it in wax combs.*

# Chapter I. Guidelines & General Considerations

Many beekeepers' associations around the world hold competitions in which honey, combs of honey, beeswax, honey bee colony products, and equipment for beekeeping are entered. Exhibitors compete in honey shows for several reasons. Some are competitive and enjoy demonstrating their abilities; others seek ribbons and trophies to display in their homes, honey houses, and sales rooms. Many wish to compare their products with those from other beekeepers and learn how to improve them. Below we discuss some things you should know before entering a honey show.

## What is honey?

There is no official government definition of honey in the United States. This is because honeys vary greatly and every definition has an exception. The original Pure Food and Drug Laws, enacted by Congress in 1906, included an official definition of honey that has only advisory status today because of the variations that may be found. This definition states that honey is "The nectar and saccharine exudations of plants gathered, modified, and stored in the comb by honeybees (*Apis*

*mellifica* and *Apis dorsata*). Honey is levorotatory and contains not more than 25 percent of water, not more than 0.25 percent of ash, and not more than 8 percent of sucrose."

While this a good, general statement it presents several problems. First, there are now six, not two, recognized species of honey bees and possibly more. A honey with 25 percent moisture will probably ferment rapidly, so this figure is too high. On the other hand, a few honeys are naturally high in moisture, perhaps even 21 or 22 percent, and should not be discriminated against in the wholesale marketplace even though they are not acceptable in a show. Dark honeys often contain more than 0.25 percent ash. It is uncommon for a honey to contain as much as 8 percent sucrose, so this figure is much too high. The above definition excludes honeydew honey, which is popular in some parts of the world. For all of these reasons, most beekeepers agree that the above definition should continue to have only advisory status. No one disputes that honey is a natural product. This means that variability exists and must be accepted. Members of the United States beekeeping industry have never condoned the production or marketing of synthetic or artificial honeys, but a few countries allow such products to be sold.

## The role of flavor in judging honey

Honey shows cannot be used to determine which honey has the best flavor because no two people have exactly the same taste buds. A judge does, however, make certain that there are no bad flavors. The flavor of a honey may be adversely affected by fermentation, bitterness, and burned sugars and proteins.

*Fermentation* — All honey contains yeast cells, which cannot grow (divide and multiply) in honey that contains less than about 19 percent water. Honey bees normally ripen honey so that it contains less than about 18 percent moisture. Several problems can arise, however, two of which are of specific concern. First, honey is hygroscopic; that is, it will pick up moisture on its surface if exposed to high humidity. Under these circumstances fermentation can occur. Second, when crystals form in honey they contain only 9.09 percent water, and the remaining water content of the liquid honey increases. If it rises above about 19 percent, fermentation may occur.

*Figure 4. Fermentation at the top of the jar resulted from high moisture and the crystallization process.*

*Bitterness* — A very small number of honeys may have a bitter taste. Honey bees cannot recognize all of the bitter tastes and flavors that humans can detect. One way to demonstrate this is to add quinine to a sugar syrup and watch the bees collect it without hesitation; the taste, which is bitter to humans, is not detectable by honey bees.

While bitterness may be a natural component of some plant nectars, bitter honeys should not be marketed or allowed into competition with normal honeys. The question of which plants are responsible for bitter honeys and how widespread they are was explored by the late Shaws of Massachusetts. They found about 40 plants that were suspected of producing bitter honey, although none appeared to do so consistently. Many of these were in the plant family Compositae. One suspected plant is sumac, but the Shaws pointed out that sumac honey is common in their area, so the problem is obviously rare. It was not determined if the bitter flavor came from the pollen, the nectar, or a contaminant (Shaw, F. R. and M. M. Shaw. Bitter honey. *Report of the State Apiarist for the Year Ending December 31, 1954.* State of Iowa. 1955).

*Burned flavor* — Honey must not have a burned flavor, although this is often difficult to avoid in dark honeys that are heated to be liquified and/or destroy yeasts. For example, it is extremely difficult to obtain a liquid buckwheat honey that does not have a slightly burned

taste. This occurs because of the high protein content of buckwheat honey. Honey is also burned when it is passed through a Brand melter, solar wax extractor, or when stored at high temperatures for a long time.

## The use of judging cards

In our opinion, a beekeeper should not enter a honey show unless the judge uses a judging card that assigns points for the various factors to be considered. The judging card should have space for the judge to make comments. A judge must demonstrate his or her competence and be willing to stand behind any decisions they make. Without a judging card one has no notion of the errors or problems that the judge encounters and that are important in making decisions. A carefully prepared and completed card should give the entrant the necessary information to improve the quality of items exhibited in a later honey show.

## Ribbons and trophies

Winning in a show is no accident. Those who win a competition should be liberally rewarded for their effort and expertise. People who have exhibited successfully are well aware that many hours of study and practice are required before one even starts to select the products and materials to be exhibited. For these reasons we suggest that those in charge of a show should not skimp. New ribbons should be printed for every show and should clearly state the name and date of the event. They should be large enough to be easily read and make a meaningful display when exhibited in a salesroom.

*Figure 5. Top class awards at an EAS show.*

We like to have a Best of Show, a very special ribbon awarded to the individual who does the best job in a show. When we judge together—one doing the cooking and the other the honey and beeswax—we usually request two Best of Show ribbons, one for each category. In our experience this is worthwhile.

## Rules for a honey show

Unfortunately, the rules and guidelines for exhibitors are not the same in all honey shows. Agreement has been reached on several points, however, and increasingly the rules are being standardized. Listed below are rules that most people agree are appropriate.

1. If an entry fee is charged, it should be the first item listed in the rules.
2. It should be stated if an entrant must belong to the society or club responsible for the show.
3. The decision(s) of the judge(s) is final.
4. All entries must be produced by the entrant in the production year, not necessarily the calendar year, in which they are exhibited.
5. Exhibitors are allowed only one entry per class. Family members may enter the same class provided that each member is responsible for the production of the entry under his or her name. (This rule is sometimes controversial.)
6. Entries must have no identifying labels or marks on the entries other than numbers or letters placed on them by the show superintendent. (Interestingly, one major honey show requires normal labels, but the show always has judges from out of state.)
7. Color grades are determined by the show superintendent, whose decision is final.
8. The show superintendent may refuse exhibits for reasons that he or she believes are just.
9. A closing time for entries should be clearly posted.
10. All entries must be exhibited in clear glass or plastic. Comb honey entries in wood may be exhibited in removable cardboard paper cartons. Round sections must have clear plastic covers and bottoms. Frames of honey and observation hives must have clear plastic or glass on both sides of the exhibit.
11. The type of jar, such as Queenline, or Gamber, may be stipulated, but this is usually not done.
12. The type of cap, metal or plastic, may be stipulated, but this is usually not done.
13. The show rules should stipulate that judging cards will be used and that these become the property of the exhibitor.
14. The show rules should stipulate the number of awards and ribbons that will be given in each class.
15. Entries usually must be left on display until a stipulated time. Unless otherwise stated, the entry remains the property of the exhibitor.

## Guidelines for the honey show superintendent

The superintendent is usually the most harried person in the arena. The contestants want to make certain their entries are handled without finger marks or other blemishes so as to present the best physical appearance to the judge. All contestants believe their entry is superior, and expect superior attention. At the same time, the superintendent must label each entry correctly and without prejudice. The superintendent should make decisions about the acceptability of jar size and shape, cap type, entry weight and so forth when the samples are delivered to his or her table.

Perhaps the best method of labeling entries is to use small gummed labels that may be attached to each entry. Each entrant is given a number, which is written on the label. The labels should be no more than half an inch in diameter. When an entry consists of two or three pieces, as with liquid honey, each piece should be given the same number. The superintendent should use an entry book to record information about the entrant and the entry.

It has been suggested that when a contestant has several entries, each should be given a separate number. For example, if an entrant has entries in the light, amber, and dark liquid classes, three different numbers would be assigned. While we don't think this is necessary, it is remotely possible that if the winner of the first liquid class judged has an entry in the next class, a judge may remember that the position won in the first class and this might affect the entrant's position in the next class. Assigning different numbers to each class takes more of the superintendent's time. It is true that if an entrant has a winning entry in one class, then his or her entry in another class should be equally good. Judges like to be consistent, and the same person continuing to win may indicate consistency on the part of the judge.

One of the most important roles played by the show superintendent is assigning liquid honey to the proper color classes. Separating comb honey color classes also may be difficult. Under no circumstances should the superintendent open a jar of honey, or take a sample, for the purpose of assigning color classes. This means that neither a Pfund grader nor any other type of color comparator may be used, and the superintendent must make decisions about color classes by eye. In no case should the entrant do anything other than suggest where the samples should be placed. This sometimes leads to conflict, especially if different samples are close in color. The entrant may believe these should be in different classes, but the decision of the superintendent must be final.

The judge assigns numerical values to the different qualities being judged and places these on the judging card. The judge usually notes the place assigned to each entry, *i.e.* first, second, etc.; and in each case the judge's decision is final. Before the judge leaves the judging room, however, each and every card and assigned position should be checked by the judge, the superintendent, or a person assigned the job and agreed to by both. Judges may resist having their addition checked, in which case they accept full responsibility for any errors made. However, it is the job of the show superintendent to double-check all entries. We suggest that a superintendent should check all cards and decisions, even after the judge has left the room and presumably completed his or her task.

The superintendent places the ribbons on the entries and usually remains in the judging room when the exhibits are opened to the public. This duty may be assigned to another person but the show must be supervised until the entrants pick up their ribbons and entries.

The final function of the superintendent is to deliver a list of the entrants and winners to the sponsoring society's secretary. Any ribbons not used in the show are likewise delivered to this person. Entry fees also may be collected by the show superintendent, in which case a report is also made to the treasurer of the society. In a few honey shows the judge serves as show superintendent. While it is possible to be objective in such cases, we suggest that judges avoid placing themselves in this position.

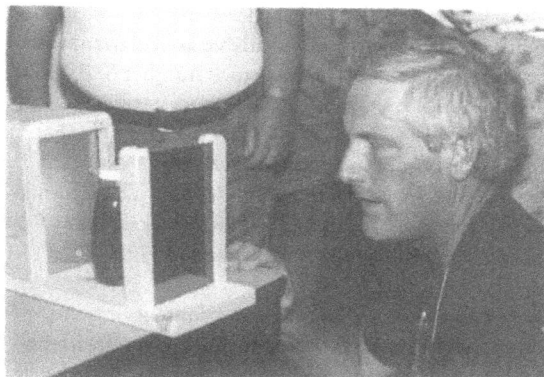

*Figure 6. Ray Allen checks a jar of honey for crystals in honey by using a polariscope.*

## Equipment for judges

Judges must be consistent both within and between shows. Some beekeepers will enter the same samples in several shows during the same year, and we do not object to this. However, a few judges do object to this practice, in part because we think that they fear their judging may not be consistent with that of other judges. To overcome this objection it is important that judges agree on what instruments should be used. Accordingly, we discuss below the gadgetry used and where to obtain further information about them.

*The polariscope* — This is our name for the gadget Dr. J. W. White Jr. devised in searching for crystals in honey. We use this name for lack of a better term; as far as we are aware, White himself gave the gadget no name other than **honey crystal detection device**. It is technically not a polariscope, which is the name for a piece of laboratory equipment used for other purposes. However, because honey show judging is not likely to overlap the use of the laboratory polariscope, we have no objection to the name.

White's gadget uses two sheets of Polaroid film, one of which is turned at a 90 degree angle to the other. The honey sample is placed between the two five or six inch square Polaroid sheets, and a shaded light source behind the two sheets gives the necessary illumination. Other objects such as lint, wax particles, and lumps of pollen grains are also easily seen using a polariscope (Figure 6 and back cover). The original paper, cited below, advises the use of "Polaroid J film", available as "Polarized filter stock number S38,495 or gray stock number S38,493" from Edmund Scientific, 101 E. Gloucester Pike, Barrington, NJ 08007. (White, J. W. Jr. and J. Maher. 1951. Detection of incipient granulation in extracted honey. *American Bee Journal* 91: 376-377. The information was reprinted in Tew, J. E. 1983. Beekeeping technology. *Gleanings in Bee Culture* 11: 577.)

*The refractometer* — The moisture content of honey (percentage of water) is determined using a refractometer. Hand-held refractometers have been developed that are accurate and easy to clean; only a drop of honey is needed to determine the moisture level. Most honey refractometers will indicate a moisture level between 12 and 25 percent with gradations of one-tenth of one percent.

Several manufacturers produce refractometers designed specifically for determining the moisture content of honey. As far as we know, all companies, both domestic and foreign, make models that read the moisture content directly. We have compared several models and found them to be remarkably accurate. In our laboratory, we have two Bausch and Lomb models that we return to the factory about every ten years to be cleaned and checked. We have not been able to determine where to send foreign models.

*The judging cards* — Most judging cards are printed on five- by eight-inch stiff "card stock" to allow enough space for the judge to make comments—the most important feature of a judging card.

It is likely that the first- and second-place winners in a honey show are as familiar with the judging process. However, beekeepers who are entering a honey show for the first time often need guidance and may be helped by reading a judge's comments about someone else's entry. One reason for judging early at a meeting is to allow others time to review the show so that they may become familiar with the process.

We prefer to see a different colored card for each show category. Yellow is an obvious choice for the beeswax exhibits; white is most frequently used for the liquid honey classes. We also suggest that each show print its own judging cards, bearing the name of the show sponsor. Some honey show winners exhibit the card along with the ribbon when they receive a high score. Photocopied cards are often not clear and do not make a favorable impression. Each category should be clearly printed on each card. However the cards are designed, the format must be consistent. For example, the place won by the entry is usually indicated in the lower right-hand portion of the card. A typical judging card is shown in Figure 7.

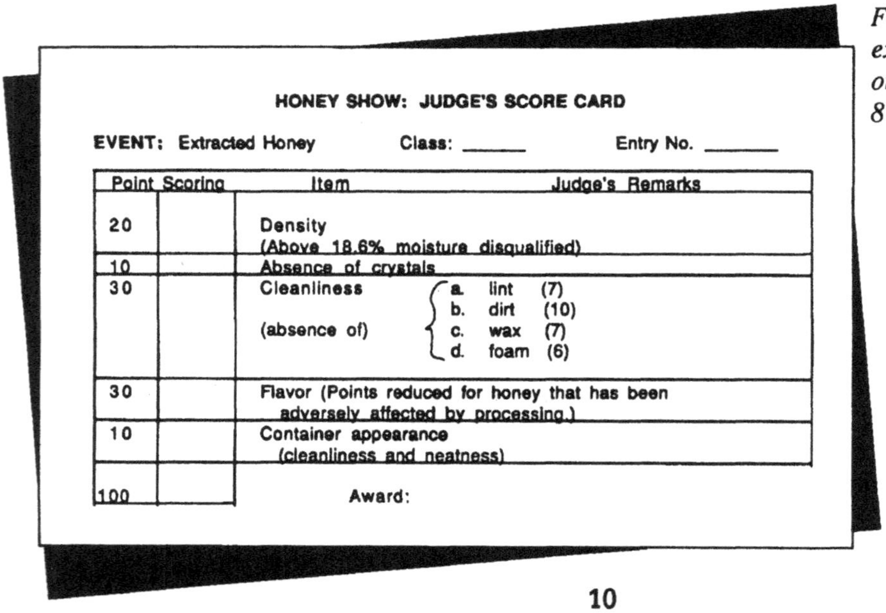

*Figure 7. Judging card for extracted honey. The original size was 5 inches x 8 inches.*

**HONEY SHOW: JUDGE'S SCORE CARD**

EVENT: Extracted Honey      Class: _____      Entry No. _____

| Point Scoring | | Item | Judge's Remarks |
|---|---|---|---|
| 20 | | Density (Above 18.6% moisture disqualified) | |
| 10 | | Absence of crystals | |
| 30 | | Cleanliness (absence of)    a. lint (7)   b. dirt (10)   c. wax (7)   d. foam (6) | |
| 30 | | Flavor (Points reduced for honey that has been adversely affected by processing.) | |
| 10 | | Container appearance (cleanliness and neatness) | |
| 100 | | Award: | |

*Figure 8. A county beekeeping association honey show.*

# Chapter 2.
# Judging Liquid Honey

An entry in a liquid honey class usually consists of three one-pound jars of liquid honey in clear glass. The reason for requesting three jars is to demonstrate if the exhibitor can be consistent. The type of jar is usually stipulated so that the entries will appear uniform in color. Honey in an oval jar may appear to be different from that in a round jar.

Liquid honey, the most important hive product in the United States, naturally constitutes the largest classes in most honey shows.

All of the honey shows we attended in the past 40 years have had only four or five classes of liquid honey, all based on color. Based on the terminology found on the Pfund grader, the classes are white, light, light amber, amber and dark. The white class is often eliminated, especially in the eastern states.

Since a show superintendent is not permitted to open a jar of honey before it is opened by the judge, the assignments of entries on the border between classes are made arbitrarily by the show superintendent or his or her representative. Unfortunately, there is no other good method. A beekeeper may make entries in all classes.

## Discussion of the judging card

The following is a discussion of the items found on most judging cards for liquid honey. The points may vary slightly, but the criteria remain the same.

## Density (Moisture content)

It is easy to determine the moisture content of liquid honey using a hand-held refractometer. There are many reasons for determining moisture, but the most important is that honey with more than 19 percent moisture may ferment. The yeasts in honey cannot grow in sugar solutions containing less than about 19 percent water because the osmotic pressure is too great. For this reason, honeys with moisture contents above 18.6 percent are disqualified in all shows. While honey in a show is usually pasteurized, opening the jar during judging, or for any other purpose, will allow airborne yeast cells to enter and possibly cause fermentation. (We do not know who determined that 18.6 percent should be the cutoff point. We suspect it was arbitrarily set by someone in the United States Department of Agriculture but experience has shown that it was a good decision).

Some controversy exists on how a judge assigns points to honeys with varying moisture contents. For example, in one show we judged recently, the judging card indicated that honeys below 16 percent moisture should be disqualified. We disagree with that rule and believe there are more important considerations. We presume that those who thought it was a good rule were considering the spreadability of the honey or its flow from a jar when on the table. In the wholesale honey trade, honeys low in moisture receive a premium because they allow the packer more flexibility in blending when preparing the honey for market. Packers often need low-moisture honey to blend with high-moisture honey. Hobby beekeepers also may blend honeys to suit themselves and their friends or customers. It is easy enough to add water to honey, but removing it is difficult and often not successful. Removing moisture may also harm the honey by driving off volatile components that are important in the makeup of its flavor.

When we judge honey, we tend to subtract more points for the qualities over which the beekeeper has the greatest control, especially crystallization, air (foam), and cleanliness. We usually award the maximum number of points to a honey with a moisture level of 16 percent or lower. We assign 19 out of 20 points to honey in the 17 percent moisture range, and 18 out of 20 points to honey in the 18 percent range (but 18.6 percent or below). This rewards beekeepers who harvest only fully ripe honey, or who know how to remove water from honey by blowing warm, dry air through a super before it is extracted. At the same time, it does not penalize 18 percent honey moisture too severely.

Measuring the moisture content of honey is a slow but routine task. Often a judge has a helper who measures and records moisture contents on the judging cards. However, the judge should be the one who writes the numerical value assigned. The show superintendent should not be designated to measure or record the moisture contents, except perhaps in small shows where there are few people to help.

In a category where three jars are required for each entry, the moisture content of only one jar is read and recorded. An entry sometimes may be made using different honeys, although this is not approved. The samples should be from the same tank. However, if an exhibitor does not enter three jars from the same batch it is usually obvious to the judge in other ways. Taking samples from three jars in order to determine an average moisture content requires too much time.

## Freedom from crystals

Liquid honey entered in a show should be free of crystals. This is because the coarse crystals that usually develop in ordinary liquid honey are unpleasant to the tongue and taste. Second, granulation changes the water content of the ungranulated portion of honey. A crystal of glucose in a liquid solution such as honey contains only a small percentage of water (9.09 percent). Because the average honey contains about 18 percent water, only

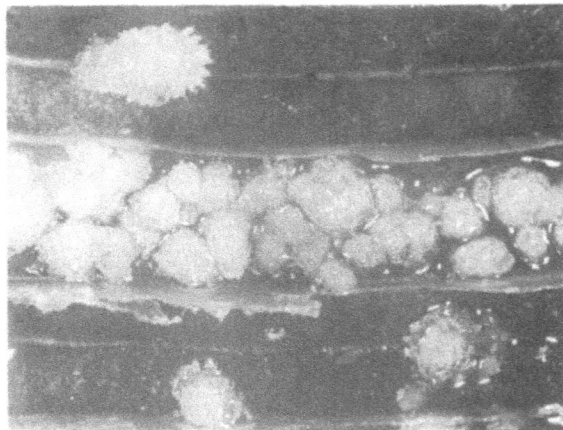

*Figure 9. Natural granulation in the comb.*

a small amount of the water present is a part of the crystal. As a result, the moisture content of the remaining liquid portion is increased.

All honeys will granulate given enough time. However, a few honeys, such as tupelo and sage, may not granulate for one or two years. Others, such as canola and aster honey, may granulate in a few weeks. All honeys are supersaturated sugar solutions, which means that granulation is inevitable. In commercial practice, honey is usually packed at or above 140 degrees F. A high temperature melts most or all of the crystal nuclei that may be present, and without a nucleus on which to grow, no crystals will form.

A small number of dust particles will bring about granulation rapidly. A simple experiment to demonstrate this is to heat some honey and cap two jars while they are still hot. After the jars have cooled to room temperature, open one jar, leave the cap off for a minute, and then recap the sample. In the case of most honeys, the jar that has had the cap removed for a minute will show signs of crystallization in a few weeks or a month, merely because dust settled onto the exposed honey.

Contestants in a honey show often enter the same samples in several shows, and we have no objection to this. Sometimes a sample that has placed well in one show may be disqualified in a later show because of partial granulation. The reason is simply that the judge in the first show opened the jars and exposed the honey to airborne dust, starting the granulation process.

*Figure 10. In the jar on the left, air bubbles were added during processing and filling. The jar on the right was filled with honey which had settled for several days, and filled carefully to avoid adding air.*

Most judges at a honey show use a polariscope, which makes any crystals clearly visible (see back cover photo). However, the first crystals that form in a jar of liquid honey are usually at the very bottom. They are, of course, much easier to see in light honey than dark honey, but a strong light may make them visible in a dark honey as well.

When honey starts to granulate, the process is usually rapid. For this reason, honey with any signs of granulation is disqualified. Judging granulation is a bit like judging moisture content. There is a sharp cutoff point, and even a small amount of granulation is not permitted. Samples with no signs of granulation receive full credit; those showing granulation are disqualified. It is a black-and-white rule.

## Cleanliness

We believe judges in a liquid honey show should concentrate their efforts on the four areas of cleanliness discussed below. Many things can go wrong in the

preparation of honey for market or a show. Honey that is exhibited should be as clean and clear.

*Lint* — Lint consists of small pieces of fiber, usually cotton, that enter the honey as it is strained. Not too many years ago it was popular for beekeepers to strain their honey through cheesecloth, and this always left a great deal of cotton lint in the honey. Nylon cloth or wire screening are best for straining honey, but wire screening is costly and difficult to clean and repair. Nylon may stretch and the holes between the strands grow large as a result of any pressure put on it. When a piece of nylon straining cloth is washed it should not be in a machine along with other types of clothing that may leave lint on the nylon.

Lint usually cannot be seen without a polariscope, and in dark honey it is usually impossible to see.

*Debris (Dirt)* — Debris in honey includes amber, brown and black specks from broken cocoons, propolis

13

and old comb. It is especially common when old combs are uncapped. Debris also may include large masses of pollen that was mixed with the honey after being thrown from uncapped cells of pollen.

Jars and caps may be covered with dust, especially if they are kept in an uncovered storage bin, and should be cleaned before the jars are filled. Glass jars are usually stored upside down in their shipping cases and are much less likely to contain debris. We know of one judge who disqualifies caps smeared with honey on the inside because he wants to check the inside of the cap for dust. In commercial packing plants most jars and caps are cleaned by a blast of air or a vacuum to remove dust before filling the jars.

Of all the considerations in a honey show, we take the presence of any specks or foreign material most seriously and heavily discount honey containing debris.

*Wax* — Since most honey is heated before it is packed, one rarely finds pieces of beeswax in a jar of honey. Unfortunately, beeswax can be easily dissolved in honey. Usually it can be detected by taste only if a large quantity is present. Dissolving beeswax in honey is not a good procedure, but it does no physical harm to the honey unless it is present in a large quantity. Beeswax melts at about 148 degrees F. Honey is often heated this high in the pasteurization process.

*Foam* — Air is incorporated into honey as it is thrown from the cells in combs and splatters onto the sides of the extractor. There is no way to avoid this problem. Air also may be incorporated by a honey pump or as the honey falls from a strainer into a tank below. Air must be removed when the honey is packed. This is best done through long-term settling. In commercial honey plants, air is removed by filtration. Air bubbles and foam, in addition to being unsightly, often contain small dust particles that may start granulation.

Air is easily detected as a ring of foam around the inside top of the jar. It may also sometimes be seen under the jar's shoulders. We discount jars of honey with foam. It is the second most serious problem after debris.

*Judging dark honey for cleanliness* — Judging dark honey for faults is difficult because one cannot see through a very dark honey, even with a polariscope. The color of amber honeys also may obscure small particles. When debris is present in honey, it usually rises to the top. One way to judge a jar of dark liquid honey is to tip it slowly and carefully about 45 degrees so that the inside of the cap is covered with about one-eighth of an inch of honey. This will be the honey off the top of the jar, and if any debris is present it should have risen to that point. It will be seen in the thin layer of honey on the cap's interior when the cap is removed and turned upside down. This is not a perfect way of judging a dark honey, but it often works reasonably well.

A second method of finding debris in dark honey is to skim and dilute a spoonful of the honey from the top of the jar. About an equal amount of water is added, shaken, and poured through a piece of fine, clean cloth. Any debris will presumably be left on the top of the cloth. This method is slow and cumbersome and not strongly advised.

## Flavor

As indicated earlier in this book, a judge does not attempt to determine which honey in a show tastes best. Flavor is a matter of preference. Just as some people prefer strong cheese, others prefer strong honey. The goal in a honey show is to eliminate honeys that have been damaged during processing or are otherwise objectionable.

Honeys that have a fermentation odor, wax flavor, or are bitter or burned should be disqualified in a show. This is another black-and-white rule. It is very difficult to prepare a sample of dark honey for a show or market without burning it to some degree because the protein present in dark honeys burns easily. In some dark, strong-tasting honeys, the burned taste may not be objectionable.

What should be done about honeydew honey? In many European countries, especially parts of Germany, Switzerland, and Poland, beekeepers are eager to produce honeydew honey, which is made from an aphid secretion. This is usually called forest honey and has a premium place on the market in countries where it is produced. Forest honey is usually produced in areas that have solid plantings of a single tree species. These tree monocultures encourage the growth and development of insects such as aphids. The aphids feed on the trees' sap, which is rich in sugar, and secrete honeydew, which is also high in sugar. Interestingly, in years when there is a good honey flow from honeydew, the colonies suffer because there is usually no pollen available and they cannot rear young bees to replace those that are foraging. Sometimes the colonies perish under these conditions because of a lack of protein.

Very little honeydew honey is produced in North America because of few forest monocultures where aphids may flourish. The honeydew that is produced is usually dark and strong and not suitable for the North American table market. As a result, it normally becomes part of a bakery blend.

When honeydew honeys are entered in a show, we suggest that the judge consult with the show superintendent and the president of the local beekeeper's society. If honeydew honey is known locally, and the beekeeper knowingly exhibited it as such, then the judge is probably bound to judge it on its other qualities. Honeydew honey may merit a separate class.

What should be done about bitter honey? Some honeys are bitter. Privet honey, for example, almost always has an objectionable taste. We suggest that, unless one has a good reason, bitter and objectionably tasting honey should be disqualified. (See Chapter 1 and "The role of flavor in judging honey.")

## Container appearance

The type and size of the jar(s) to be used in a honey show should be specified in the show rules. It is unfair to competitors when various types of jars are used since different jars may affect the color and other qualities of the product they contain.

The physical appearance of a container is a consideration when one buys a jar of honey or other food product. As a result, it is also a consideration in a honey show. Glass jars used for showing honey should be free of blemishes, lines, or deformities resulting from their manufacture because these may distract the judge or another viewer as the package is examined.

Metal jar caps should be free of scratches, dents, or other visibly objectionable features. Many exhibitors use plastic caps because they are more uniform and less likely to contain defects. There has been some discussion about specifying whether or not exhibitors should use plastic or metal caps, but we see no good reason for doing so. We do not object to having both types of caps in the same class in a show.

# Chapter 3. Crystallized Honey

An entry in the finely granulated honey class usually consists of three one-pound clear glass jars or tubs of crystallized honey. The reason for using clear glass is discussed below.

When judging crystallized honey it is important to understand why it is made. The reasons are simple: it is dripless, has a long shelf life, and an excellent flavor.

The process for making finely granulated honey was developed and patented by the late Professor E. J. Dyce of Cornell University in 1935 (see Morse, R. A. 1983. The Dyce process for making crystallized honey. *Gleanings in Bee Culture* 111: 441-442).

## Color

Crystallized honey is always lighter in color than its liquid counterpart. The reason for this is that when honey granulates, the crystals are formed by the sugar glucose, not the fructose. (These two sugars are present in more or less equal quantities in honey.) Glucose

*Figure 11. Gamber honey jar.*

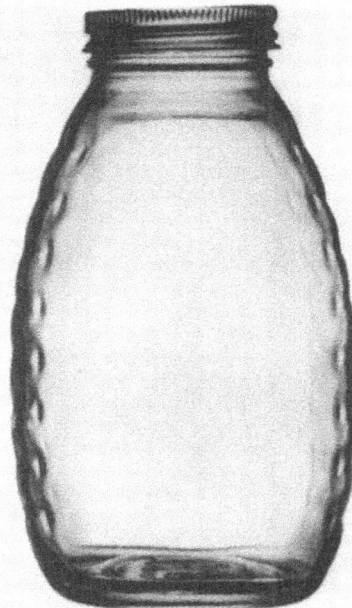

crystals are white. No matter how firm the crystallized honey becomes, the glucose crystals are surrounded by fructose and water. However, many of the glucose crystals lie on the surface—thus the light color. Because the amount of glucose in a honey may vary, the degree to which the honey sample is lightened also varies. For this reason, honey color is not a consideration in the crystallized class.

## Clear glass

When crystallized honey is made, it shrinks slightly and may pull away from the side of the container. Under these circumstances, the white glucose crystals may give the surface an odd, or at least a different, appearance. In fact, some consumers believe the honey is moldy. For this reason, those who pack crystallized honey use opaque tubs or jars. A reasonably satisfactory alternative is to use a full wraparound label on a clear glass or plastic jar.

However, because a judge must be able to see the honey, the rules state that for show purposes crystallized honey must be packed in clear glass. Judges understand how honey is physically affected by crystallization and must not discount samples in which the honey has pulled away from the side of the jar.

*Figure 12. Crystallized or creamed honey.*

## Discussion of the judging card

The following is a discussion of the items found on most judging cards for crystallized honey.

## Fineness of crystals

Beekeepers and consumers who have been asked generally agree that finely granulated honey has more taste appeal than honey with large, coarse crystals. The crystals in properly made crystallized honey should be so tiny, that when a small amount of the honey is pushed against the roof of the mouth with the tongue, one cannot feel the crystals. In other words, the consistency of properly made crystallized honey should resemble that of butter. Coarse crystals are hard to dissolve, which also gives them less taste appeal.

## Degree of uniformity and firmness

Newly made crystallized honey is almost rock hard and difficult to spread with a knife. Honey granulates most rapidly at 57 degrees F., but it is neither practical nor desirable to store or use honey at that temperature. After the crystallized honey is made, it must be brought to room temperature so that it is spreadable. Another serious problem is that if the honey becomes too warm, some of the crystals may liquefy, at least partially. Partially liquefied crystallized honey should be heavily discounted .

Commercial packers of crystallized honey adjust the moisture content of their honey (usually through blending). In warm climates, a honey to be used for crystallization should have about one-half percent less moisture than that packed for cool climates. Those who exhibit in summer honey shows may take this into consideration and enter a honey with a slightly lower moisture content.

## Degree of cleanliness and freedom from foam

The light color of crystallized honey makes it easy to detect specks of comb and other debris. As in the case of liquid honey, debris, especially specks of dark wax, is discounted.

Various methods are used to mix seed crystals into liquid honey in order to force granulation. This often involves using paddles or a pump, both of which almost invariably add air in the form of fine bubbles. If the crystallized honey is not cooled rapidly, these air bubbles will rise to the top and appear as foam. Commercially, this is circumvented by cooling the seeded honey rapidly, or by allowing it to become partially crystallized and homogenizing it before it is placed in the final container and becomes firm.

Crystallized honey with foam on top of the pack must be heavily discounted or even disqualified if too much foam is present.

### Flavor: absence of off-flavors, overheating, and fermentation

As in the case of liquid honey, off-flavors and burning of honey usually are easy to detect and are considered accordingly.

Crystallized honey can sometimes ferment. As discussed above, when a glucose crystal forms in honey it contains 9.09 percent water, about half the normal glucose to water ratio in honey since honey contains about 18 percent moisture. As a result, the liquid fraction of the honey, which is present even when the honey appears to be firmly granulated, is increased. If the honey is pasteurized, any yeast cells are killed. If it is not pasteurized and the water content of the honey rises above about 19 percent, the honey may ferment. Pasteurization is part of the Dyce method of making crystallized honey and is an important consideration. Any fermented samples of honey should be disqualified in a show. Other off-flavors, including overheating, the presence of a beeswax flavor, and bitterness, are treated as in other classes.

# Chapter 4.
# Comb Honey

An entry in the comb honey class usually consists of three pieces or sections of comb.

Producing comb honey is an art requiring special equipment and a much more intensive colony management scheme than the production of liquid honey. Premium sections of comb honey can be produced only in areas with good honey flows. For all of these reasons, the production of comb honey is waning.

Before the enactment of the Pure Food and Drug Laws in 1906, many beekeepers in the United States produced comb honey. They did so because the public had greater confidence in its purity. There was much adulteration and mislabeling of honey (and other food products) at the time; that's why and the Pure Food and Drug laws were needed. During the First and Second World Wars there was increased pressure and financial incentive to produce as much honey as possible because of sugar rationing. Only a few decades ago, many beekeepers still made a full-time living producing comb honey. As far as we are aware, no one in the United States does so today. However, comb honey classes at honey shows continue to be popular. They represent a great challenge to those who enjoy competition because so many things can go wrong in its production.

Judging comb honey differs in several ways from judging liquid honey. Comb honey has traditionally been produced in square or rectangular wooden

*Figure 13. Top Left - Basswood section comb honey. Top and bottom right - Cut comb honey. Bottom left - Round comb honey.*

*Figure 14. Half comb honey cassettes. Special care and effort is needed to produce comb honey in any container.*

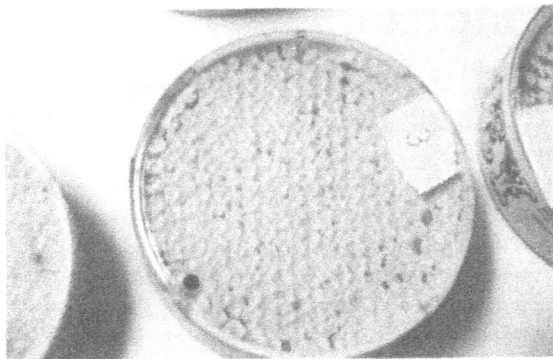

*Figure 15. Even one open cell detracts from the white cappings of round section honey.*

sections; both contain 12 to 14 ounces of honey. In most states, a comb honey package is sold as a unit, not by weight; thus, unlike the weight of a jar of liquid honey, scant attention is paid to the weight of a section of comb honey, except in states where it is required by law. Because there is little difference between square and rectangular sections, they are usually entered in the same class. The class may be divided into two parts: one for light-colored honey sections and one for dark sections.

*Round sections*—Round plastic comb honey sections were invented in the mid-1950s and have become more popular than wooden sections for several reasons. A round section contains only seven or eight ounces of honey and is therefore filled more quickly by the bees. Bees do not care to fill the corners of square or rectangular sections, but will often do a perfect job filling a round section. The round section furniture that holds the sections in place is designed in such a way that bees use very little propolis. Also important is that the smooth surface of the plastic reduces the bee's inclination to cover it with propolis. The near absence of propolis reduces the time required to prepare a round section for market. For these reasons, too, it is easier to produce round sections. They should not be judged in competition with wooden sections. Judging round sections is a little more difficult because they usually have fewer faults. As in the case of wooden sections, the round section class may be divided into two parts based on honey color.

*Half combs*—Half combs are a recent innovation. They are plastic trays with raised cell patterns, coated with beeswax, on the bottom and as part of the tray. There is no midrib—only half of a comb. Half combs are simple to package for market because it is necessary only to remove the tray from the section super and to snap a cover into place. Because they have been seen in competitions, they may deserve a special class in a show.

## Discussion of the judging card

The following is a discussion of the items found on most judging cards for comb honey including wooden, round, and half comb sections.

## Uniformity of appearance

It is expected that the three sections will be as similar as possible. This is usually achieved by producing the sections on the same colony or at least the same apiary where the bees forage on the same plant(s). Having identical sections is, of course, not possible.

Additionally, each section itself should be uniform. If one section contains honeys of different colors, it will usually be disqualified. Color is considered sufficiently important in grading comb honey that it is discussed here and separately below. The comb surface should be uniformly level from one side to the other and from top to bottom. The cappings and other physical features of the comb should be the same. The best, most uniform comb honey sections are produced during a rapid, intense honey flow. The quality of the comb honey section super furniture is important. Furniture with broken parts may cause bees to draw (extend) cells out from the comb further. This may give the comb surface a bumpy appearance. Such combs are, of course, not uniform.

The wood that is used to make wooden sections should be uniform in appearance. This is one reason why basswood is used almost exclusively to make sections; it is almost always the same color. The wood should not have any blemishes, dark streaks or other features which distract from the section's overall appearance.

## Absence of uncapped cells

Honey bees evolved in nests in hollow trees that are usually shaped like a tall cylinder. That is why bees usually avoid square corners in a man-made hive. Thus, obtaining square or rectangular sections of comb honey that are filled to their capacity is difficult except when there is a populous colony and an intense, rapid nectar flow. On the other hand, we frequently see round sections that are filled and have no empty or uncapped cells (Figure 15).

In some honey shows we have been forced to count the number of uncapped cells in order to make a final decision. For example, a section with one to five open or empty cells, including those in the corners, is given a higher value than one with six to ten open cells, etc.

When bees in a colony are smoked, many of them will engorge on honey. If these smoked bees are in a comb honey super with filled and capped sections, the bees will make small openings in the cappings to obtain honey. This defaces the section. You should not smoke bees in a comb honey super or use smoke to remove bees from a comb honey super. We usually do not discount a section with such opened cells in this category, but more frequently in the cleanliness category for reasons discussed below.

## Uniformity of color

The color of the honey in a section of comb should be uniform; that is, the section should contain only one kind of honey or a uniform blend of the same honeys. Some people argue that a comb of honey may contain two or three honeys of different colors and still be a natural product. This is true. However, when faced with a question of this nature, we fall back on the rule or question, "Will it confuse a customer?" The answer is generally yes, and for this reason sections with honey of different colors should be discounted heavily or even disqualified.

## Watery cappings

When the wax over honey-filled cells lie on or against the honey they have a watery appearance. There is nothing wrong with the honey or its flavor when watery cappings are present. It is merely more appealing for comb honey sections to have clean, white cappings built over the honey so that they do not touch it. This opinion has been expressed in bee journals and bee books for the past century and we concur. The difference is especially noticeable when bees build cappings over a very dark honey, such as buckwheat, in which case the white cappings give the section an especially fine appearance against the dark background.

*Figure 16. Watery cappings may be natural or a result of the hygroscopic nature of honey.*

Watery cappings on comb honey occur for two reasons. First, honey is hygroscopic; that is, if the humidity is high the honey will pick up moisture at its surface. This increases its volume and the honey may press against the cappings. If the humidity in the storage area is sufficiently high, the sections may weep, that is, droplets of water will exude through the cappings and will be visible on the surface. The wax cappings that bees build over cells of honey are not air- or watertight. Comb honey should be stored where it is warm and dry. Some beekeepers use a dehumidifier to reduce the humidity in the area where they keep their comb honey. Sections that weep should be heavily discounted.

The second reason for watery cappings is because of the bees' genetics. One hundred years ago, beekeepers selected bees that left an airspace between the honey and the cappings. This was just one of many considerations comb honey producers made when selecting stock for comb honey production. Since most beekeepers produce liquid honey today, the question of watery cappings and how to control them through the selection of breeding stock is usually discussed only at honey shows.

When a judge finds watery cappings for this second reason, the question of how to judge an entry becomes more difficult. Because comb honey sections with white cappings have greater eye appeal, we are inclined to remove points when we find watery cappings for either reason. However, if sections are weeping because they were not stored properly we subtract more points. A judge may disqualify wooden sections that are weeping so much that honey runs down their faces and sticks to the cardboard or plastic container in which they are packaged. Today, it is rare to find sections of comb honey that do not have some watery cappings. (Pictures of sections with few or no watery cappings may be found in some of the older bee journals and bee books such as Dr. C. C. Miller's *Fifty Years Among the Bees*. 1920. A. I. Root Company, Medina, Ohio).

## Cleanliness of sections

As for many other classes in a honey show, cleanliness is probably the most important consideration in judging comb honey. We are concerned with the cleanliness of both the wood or plastic that surrounds the comb and the comb surface itself.

Wooden comb honey sections are made of basswood lumber, which stains easily. When propolis is deposited on the wood it will penetrate sufficiently so that the stain cannot be removed. Comb honey sections are carefully sanded to reduce the amount of propolis the bees will collect and deposit on them, but the amount of propolis a colony of bees collects can only be reduced, never eliminated. Many years ago, comb honey producers routinely coated the exposed tops of their wooden sections with hot paraffin or beeswax applied with a small brush. The sections were waxed after the supers were assembled. Before the section was sold or exhibited, most of the paraffin was scraped off with a knife, leaving a clean, white wooden top. A section stained with propolis is a serious distraction, and stained sections are discounted accordingly.

Basswood lumber sometime contains streaks and blemishes. This has already been discussed under the question of uniformity but deserves mention here too. The sections used for show purposes should be carefully selected so that that judge will not subtract points.

Round plastic sections have an advantage regarding propolis deposition. Because of this, a small amount of propolis on a round ring is often discounted more than the same amount of propolis on a wooden section.

The cleanliness of the comb surface in a comb honey class is very important. Travel stain is the greatest offender. Most travel stain is caused by pollen-laden bees walking across the comb surface and accidentally leaving a pollen residue. For this reason there should be no upper entrances in supers containing comb honey sections. Pollen-laden bees should be forced to walk into

the bottom entrance of the hive and deposit their loads in the brood nest area. In this way, they cannot cause travel stain in the honey storage area. Propolis will cause the same problems.

Bits of smoker soot on a comb surface are discounted heavily. One should not apply smoke when removing a comb honey section super. Beekeepers often fail to recognize how much soot from a smoker is blown into a bee hive when they are making a colony examination. The bees remove this with ease, but it takes time. As a test, one may puff some smoke against a white painted surface to see the great amount of soot that is expelled from a smoker.

As mentioned above, the greatest problem in using smoke to remove comb honey sections is that bees will engorge when smoked. If these bees are on the surface of the comb honey section, they will make small holes in the cappings. These holes will be repaired, usually within 24 hours, if the section super is not removed. Small holes caused by feeding bees may be discounted here or under the section pertaining to uniformity.

A judge is always alert to the possible presence of wax moths and *Braula coeca* larvae in comb honey sections. The presence of either is a serious fault that may lead to disqualification.

## Freedom from granulation and pollen

Granulation in comb honey, as in the case of liquid honey, is a serious fault and usually is grounds for disqualification. However, granulation is much more difficult to detect in comb honey. A judge can make a visual assessment only. He or she has the right to open individual cells and remove some of the honey for a taste test if there is a question. The best protection against granulation is to store the sections of honey in a freezer.

A cell of pollen in a section of comb honey is sufficient reason for some judges to disqualify the entry. If one thinks in terms of a consumer, such a position is easily justified. How, indeed, is a consumer to know what a cell of pollen is, let alone how to cope with it? Most pollen is bitter to taste. The presence of one cell of pollen in one of the three sections in a show entry may be reason to discount the entry heavily, but does not necessarily constitute grounds for disqualification. A total of two or more cells of pollen in the three sections is probably grounds for disqualification.

### Uniformity of weight

In most states, comb honey is sold as a unit and not by weight. As a result, most judges do not weigh entries. However, the sections in an exhibit of three should be as uniform in weight as possible. In honey shows in states where the weight of a section of comb honey must be marked on the container, the judge should take weight into consideration and ensure that the sections have the minimum weight indicated.

### Total weight of entry

This category, as well as the preceding, is pertinent only in states where law demands the listing of the weight of a section. Information about this consideration should be posted in the rules for the benefit of the exhibitors and judges.

*Figure 17. Cut comb honey in plastic boxes.*

# Chapter 5.
# Cut Comb Honey

An entry in the cut comb honey class usually consists of three pieces of comb cut from a standard full- or half-depth frame and placed in plastic trays. Individual pieces of comb usually weigh between 12 and 16 ounces. Cut comb honey is different from chunk honey, which is one or more pieces of comb placed in a widemouthed jar and surrounded by liquid honey.

### Discussion of the judging card

The following items are usually found on a judging card for cut comb honey. The judging of cut comb honey deserves a separate card; the standard cards used for judging comb or chunk honey may be modified and used.

### Neatness of cut

Exhibitors of cut comb honey have the advantage of being able to cut out or around empty and uncapped cells and other defects. The exhibit may suffer from the way the cut is made and the fact that the midrib of the comb is exposed. The cuts should be parallel and uniform and the pieces of comb should be the same size. No bits or pieces of beeswax should be left on the comb or in the tray.

### Depth of cells and straightness of foundation

The cells on both sides of the midrib should be the same depth. The foundation should be straight, not wavy. Wavy foundation is a serious problem for cut comb and chunk honey producers because it reduces eye appeal. Beeswax comb foundation expands and contracts as the temperature changes. It is best to put the foundation into the supers the day they are placed on the colony. That, of course, is not possible for commercial producers and is often too much of a nuisance for those who produce only one or two supers of cut comb honey. If the supers containing foundation are made up before the honey flow, they should be stored where the temperature is as uniform as possible in order to reduce the changes that occur as the foundation expands and contracts.

### Draining cut comb sections

Liquid honey should not be present on the bottom of the plastic tray in which the pieces of cut comb honey are placed. A chief reason for this is that the liquid honey has been exposed to air and dust and may granulate long before the honey in the comb.

Pieces of comb may be drained by placing them in an extractor sling and revolving the extractor at a very slow speed. A drawback of this method is that the wire on the bottom of the sling may leave marks on one side of the comb. If the extractor is run too fast, some of the wax cappings may be broken.

The most common draining method is to place the pieces of cut comb on a wire-bottomed tray and leave them in a warm room for several hours until the free honey on the sides of the comb drains away.

### Other considerations

In addition to the above qualities, pieces of cut comb honey are judged on the presence of travel stain, uniformity of the surface, cells of pollen, open cells, opening of cappings by smoked bees, soot, and all of the considerations used when comb honey is judged.

# Chapter 6.
# Chunk Honey

An entry in the chunk honey class normally consists of pieces of comb, usually in three widemouthed one-pound jars, surrounded by liquid honey. However, we have seen shows in which one three-pound widemouthed jar was exhibited, usually with two or three pieces of comb.

Chunk honey has great visual and taste appeal. Chunk honey originated in the southeastern states, especially Georgia and Florida, many years ago. The favorite liquid honey most often used is gallberry, which has a fine flavor, good color, and is slow to granulate. Clover honey is sometimes used in the northern states, but it is susceptible to early granulation. The seed crystals are usually on the exterior of the comb, especially where the comb has been cut and not drained. A crystallized or partially crystallized package has little eye appeal, and the coarse crystals that develop are not pleasant to taste.

In most honey shows, a special judging card is used for chunk honey. The liquid portion of a chunk honey pack should be checked for moisture content with the usual rules applying. All of the remaining rules used to judge liquid and comb honey classes also apply. It is because these two classes overlap that a special judging card is needed. Pieces of comb may sometimes be found on the surface of the liquid honey as a result of cutting the comb.

# Chapter 7.
# Bulk Frames of Honey

An entry in the bulk honey frame class usually consists of a single comb of honey in a standard wooden frame, contained in a suitable carrying case. In recent years we have seen a few beekeepers exhibiting bulk frames made partially or wholly of plastic. We try to avoid plastic bee equipment in our own operation, but have no objection to others exhibiting such frames.

The bulk frame class may be subdivided into "frames to be extracted" and "frames to be used for cut comb honey". Half-depth frames usually are judged separately from full-depth frames. The class may be divided into light and dark color classes. The judging card is the same as that used to judge comb honey. In fact, some cards will read "Comb Honey and Bulk Honey Frame." It is understood that only combs with new foundation will be entered.

*Figure 18. A bulk frame of honey at EAS honey show.*

A class that was once popular in Ontario (Canada) honey shows, and perhaps elsewhere, was the "heaviest bulk honey frame". Weight was the only consideration. We have heard a description of the technique used for making a frame heavier, but have never done it ourselves. To add weight to a frame, one needs an especially good honey flow and a strong colony of bees. Once the flow is in progress, the super with the bulk honey frame(s) is opened every day and the frames moved another one-eighth or one-quarter inch apart. This must be done just before the bees cap the cells. How far apart the frames are moved each day depends upon the rapidity of the honey flow and the beekeeper's ability to judge that factor. As the frames are moved apart, the bees continue to respect bee space and draw the cells out a bit further. We understand it is possible to force the bees to build cells two or more inches deep. Obviously a frame with cells this deep on both sides will contain a great deal of honey. Transporting such a frame to a show is a difficult matter!

*Figure 19. This beeswax figure reflects the skill of person who molded and finished it.*

# Chapter 8. Beeswax

An entry in the beeswax class usually consists of a block of wax weighing at least two pounds. Beeswax was humanity's first plastic. We have seen lists of hundreds of uses for beeswax including waxing a thread for sewing, wax tablets, waterproofing, in sealants, and making seals. The list seems to be almost endless.

Beeswax contains over 300 individual chemical components. This variability makes it difficult to define because there is no official or government definition. Beeswax buyers rely chiefly on color, odor, and taste in in order to determine its value. However, when beeswax is secreted by honey bees it is white, odorless, and tasteless. The contaminants, especially propolis and pollen, give beeswax many of its unique physical and chemical characteristics. These same contaminants, especially the propolis, give beeswax candles their unique odor when they are burned. Because of all of these variables, judging beeswax and beeswax products is often difficult.

Working with molten beeswax can be dangerous. It is wise to mention a few precautions. An open flame should never be used to heat beeswax because it may catch fire. Also, if the beeswax contains any water, the whole mass may foam violently when the water reaches its boiling point. (Water can be dissolved in beeswax). Beeswax will burn fiercely when it reaches its flash point, which is 490 to 525 degrees F.

Excellent beeswax can be obtained using a solar wax extractor. However, solar wax extractors are not efficient in removing wax from old comb and cappings. Solar wax extractors are safe and rarely reach more than 190 degrees F. Blocks of wax may be reheated and liquefied in a solar wax extractor with ease.

## Discussion of the judging card

The following is a discussion of the items found on most judging cards used for beeswax entries.

## Color

Beeswax in a show should be light yellow and bright. The best color is perhaps best described as canary yellow. When we judge a beeswax class, we select the block that we believe has the greatest eye appeal and judge the others against it. We may not give this best colored block a full score of 30—the figure assigned to color on most judging cards—but try to find a value based on past experience. We have judged shows where two and sometimes three blocks of wax may have slightly different colors, but all still have good color. There is a wide range of suitable yellow colors.

## Cleanliness

There are a variety of ways to clean wax. Commercially, of course, it is filtered under pressure with diatomaceous earth. Many exhibitors remove debris by allowing their wax to pass through thick cloth filters. This is a slow, difficult process that unfortunately leaves much beeswax in the cloth; this may, however, be removed by boiling the filter.

When beeswax is in a liquid state, any dirt that is present will settle to the bottom. Settling takes time and should not be rushed. Rarely does any light material settle to the top, but if it does, it is easily skimmed off. Many beekeepers obtain clean wax by pouring the wax off the top of the container in which it is liquefied. Yet another method is to allow a cake of wax containing debris to cool slowly, thus trapping the debris on the bottom where it may be cut away. After the debris is removed, the block of clean wax may be remelted and cast in the final mold.

Cleanliness in beeswax also refers to freedom from bad odors. Sometimes the honey in beeswax refuse, cappings, and old comb, can ferment. A fermentation odor in beeswax is difficult to remove or mask and beeswax smelling of fermentation should be judged harshly.

Because debris in beeswax settles to the bottom, it is easy to see. The judge merely turns the cake of wax upside down and counts any specks that are present.

## Uniformity of appearance

If a block of beeswax is cooled too rapidly, layering marks may show along the sides. Bubbles are sometimes also seen. These are not desirable and cause the sample to lose points. The mold used to cast the final block should be free of dents, scratches, ridges, numbers, or names imprinted in the block. Most beekeepers use rectangular or round molds, but no one type is required. The wax should be poured into the mold all at once in order to avoid layering marks.

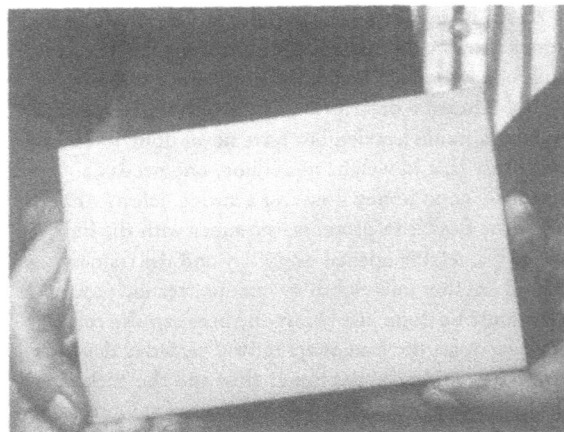

*Figure 20. A light-colored, well cleaned block of beeswax ready for show.*

## Cracking and shrinking

When beeswax cools and becomes solid, it loses about ten percent of its volume. If the wax is cooled too rapidly, huge cracks will be seen along the top surface or it may be concave. Beekeepers often warm an ordinary kitchen oven, turn off the heat, and place the mold containing the liquid wax inside. Ovens are insulated and hold heat for as much as 12 hours. Beeswax should never be heated in an oven because the temperature may reach the flash point and an explosion may occur. However, beeswax in a previously heated oven cools slowly, and cracks usually do not appear. Likewise, wax may be liquefied in an insulated solar wax extractor that is subsequently covered with blankets in order to retain the heat and the whole mass allowed to cool slowly.

Beeswax may be dissolved in honey, and honey and water may dissolve in beeswax. For these reasons it is sometimes necessary for the judge to break off a corner of the wax cake and do a taste test. Although this ruins the cake of wax for another show, judges have every right to make this test.

# Chapter 9.
# Observation Hives

An entry in the observation hive class consists of a single hive, usually with one or two standard full-depth combs. One comb is above the other if a two-frame hive is entered. Larger hives are usually discouraged because size adds little to the display and increases the chance that the hive may be overturned.

We do not remember ever seeing a judging card for observation hives, but we have consulted with several colleagues and outlined the points we think are important:

| | |
|---|---|
| Special features | 40 |
| Cleanliness and general appearance | 20 |
| Construction and suitability of the carrying case | 20 |
| Physical condition of the frame(s) and hive | 20 |

## Special features

An observation hive should be more than a glass-walled box containing comb covered with bees. It may be used to demonstrate many aspects of honey bee biology and colony life. For example, is the queen marked with paint or a colored disc? Are some workers and drones marked? If all three are marked, different colors might be used so that they are distinct. Is there a card or small poster describing the marked bees?

An observation hive may be made up with comb honey sections on top of a brood frame. These may be in different stages of construction. Alternatively, one may use a sheet of foundation in a full- or half-depth frame to illustrate wax secretion and comb building. The varnishing with propolis by the bees may be explained and illustrated.

The width, or the space between the two glass panes of the hive, may vary depending upon the purpose for which the hive is designed, and this must be judged accordingly. Most factory-made observation hives have two inches between the glass walls. However, the normal spacing between comb midribs in a super of combs is only one and a half inches. The reason for a wide spacing in a factory-made observation hive is that there is room for more bees in a layer nearly two or three deep over the comb surface. A greater number of bees can more easily maintain a normal brood rearing temperature of 94 to 96 degrees F. In the cool of the night this may be important. However, a wide spacing with more bees, also makes it difficult to see the comb and its contents. To illustrate brood rearing, including the egg laying pattern and brood feeding, the hive must be wide enough for only one bee over the comb surface. For experimental purposes, we often make observation hives narrow so that hive activities are easily seen. In such a situation, it is important to place some kind of insulation over the hive when it is not in use in order to help the bees protect their brood in cool weather. Various types of blankets made of cloth, Styrofoam®, or plastic have been devised.

## Cleanliness and general appearance

At a honey show, observation hives are usually screened and the bees have no opportunity to fly or clean the hive. This means that debris or dead bees may accumulate on the bottom of the hive. The judge must allow for a reasonable amount of debris, but it should be kept to a minimum. The exhibitor should arrange for the bees in the hive to have flight up to the evening before the show. With luck, the weather will cooperate.

*Figure 21. An observation hive allows the public to view bee behavior close-up, like food sharing.*

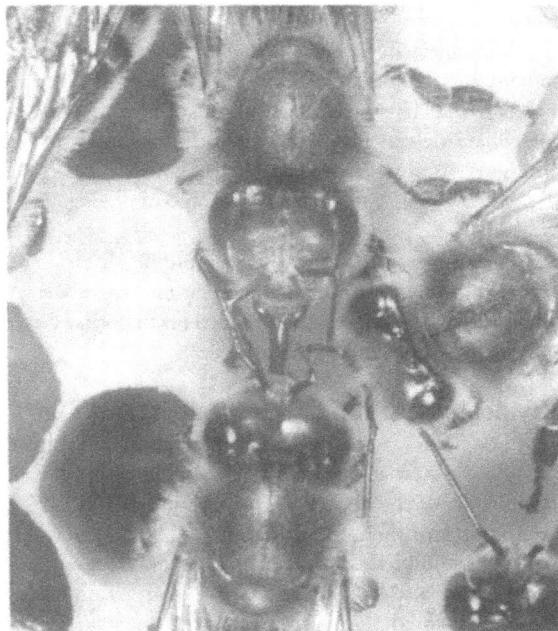

Figure 22. Beeswax flowers formed into an arrangement makes a nice novelty item.

# Chapter 10. Novelties

It is difficult if not impossible to make suggestions about judging a novelty class. Novelties may be anything related to the beekeeping industry, but beyond this there are no special requirements. We have seen honey pot collections, bee buttons and jewelry exhibited. Items made from beeswax are a favorite in the novelty class. A beeswax novelty, such as a special candle or wax figure, is judged as if it were beeswax, except that a certain value must be added for the novelty of the exhibit. Under such circumstances it is difficult to use a standard judging card, but some notes left for the exhibitor and the audience are worthwhile.

Figure 23. A decorative item made from beeswax— just one type of entry in the novelty class.

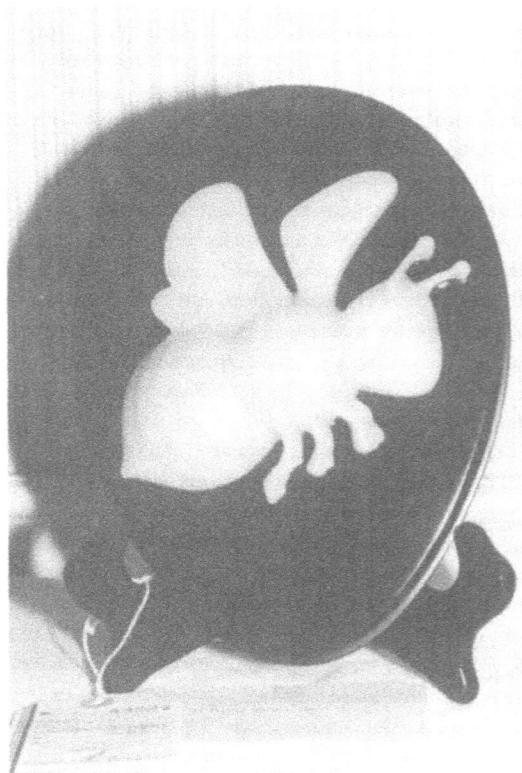

## Construction and suitability of the carrying case

It is especially important that an observation hive be constructed so that bees will not escape even if the hive is jarred. This is particularly true of hives in county fairs where viewers frequently touch and feel the products. An observation hive should have a base as wide as six or eight inches to protect it from being overturned.

The entire inside of the hive should be visible. The corners in some factory-made observation hives are sometimes obscured because of wood on the outer face, and one cannot see all of the interior.

## Physical condition of the frame(s) and hive

The frame(s) and wax comb in an observation hive should be as new as possible. There should be little propolis inside the hive. The hive exterior should be painted or varnished. In our opinion, light-colored, varnished wood has the best physical appearance. However, we also have seen attractive observation hives that were painted.

# Chapter 11. Beekeepers' Gadgets

An entry in the gadget class may be any item related to the beekeeping industry and of possible value to a beekeeper. A written explanation accompanying the entry should not be necessary, but may be helpful in explaining how, when, and where the gadget may be used.

Many beekeepers are gadgeteers and often invent or reinvent useful tools for use in the apiary. Creating a card for judging gadgets is difficult because gadgets vary so much. We doubt if it is possible to construct a card that covers everything important. Thus, we list only some of the questions that come to a judge's mind as gadgets are reviewed.

We have no objection to a gadget that does not represent a new idea. In fact, considering the age of our industry, it is difficult to find many new things. It should be remembered that one purpose of a honey show is to educate other beekeepers; and because no homemade gadget is exactly like its predecessor, it is in many ways new. For example, although hive lifters are invented again and again they are important and can save a great deal of back strain. They are therefore worthy of being entered and judged in a gadget show. There are a number of variations in the ways they may be made.

The following are some of the many considerations used in judging gadgets: usefulness, cost, ease of construction, durability, and ease of storage (or carrying to the apiary).

# Chapter 12. Mead (Honey Wine)

An entry in the mead class usually consists of a single clear glass bottle of honey wine with a proper closure. An entry in the sparkling mead class must be in a bottle whose closure will withstand high pressure; this bottle may be tinted.

The honey wine class is usually divided into the following categories: light and dark dry, light and dark sweet, honey-fruit wine, and sparkling. Since there are usually few entries in the sparkling class, it is normally not subdivided further. Spiced meads have never been popular in the United States, although they are often found in Europe. It someday may be necessary to create a category for them.

### Discussion of the judging card

The following items are found on most judging cards used for mead.

### Color

The color of mead must be attractive. Pale white and murky brown are unsuitable colors that do little, if anything, to stimulate taste appeal. Usually only a few points are assigned to the color character because other considerations are obviously more important.

### Clarity

Bottles of old wines, especially reds, often contain deposits (sediments). In such wines their presence is

*Figure 24. Ribbons on winning bottles of mead.*

understood and acceptable. However, in the case of mead, there is a very serious problem regarding the slow deposition of protein as the product ages. This has little or no effect on the flavor but gives the mead a hazy, unacceptable appearance. There are several ways to avoid this problem, and it is the judge's duty to penalize meads that are not clear.

## Bouquet, odor, and aroma

Whenever one opens any bottle of an alcoholic beverage, a bouquet should be released that tingles the senses and entices one to proceed with the sampling. It is difficult to describe a proper bouquet, although once it is experienced it stays in the mind.

Bad odors can emanate from mead. The foul smell of an acetic acid fermentation is easily detected. Moldy barrels can cause bad odors. If the wrong yeast is used, or a mead is too young, there will no bouquet or a yeasty odor. Bottles that are not properly closed will reveal themselves when first opened.

## Flavor, balance, and quality

In the final analysis, a mead must taste good and encourage the drinker to sample the product a second time. If there is no desire for a second taste, the mead fails this test. Meads, like all alcoholic beverages, may be too young, too old, too bland, too tart, too acidic, or otherwise lack appeal. Judges are very aware that sugar

*Figure 25. Considerable effort goes into mead making—a second price in a national show is reason to celebrate!*

or spices are often used to cover up bad tastes, and they must be alert to see through such disguises. Unfortunately, the public often thinks that any product made from honey must be sweet. Some of the very best meads are dry with no residual sugar.

## Container

A bottle of mead must be properly corked or capped to protect against infection and oxygen that may destroy its delicate flavor.

If a cork is used, it must be properly seated; that is, properly placed in the neck of the bottle. The top of the cork should be about an eighth of an inch below the top of the bottle. The cork should be one-and-a-half to two inches long and have been designed for closing wine bottles. A secondhand cork is not acceptable. When a cork is used, the neck of the bottle must not be tapered or flared, but the sides must be parallel for the distance occupied by the cork. Bottles that are used for many alcoholic beverages have their insides tapered outward, and the corks cannot fill the spaces properly or offer the necessary protection that they should.

Corks used to bottle sparkling beverages are designed differently and require a special machine to seat them properly. Plastic corks designed for sparkling beverages appear to work well, although a judge may have a prejudice against plastic because it is not in keeping with tradition. However, one cannot discriminate unless the type of cork is indicated in the show rules. The cork in a bottle of sparkling mead should be wired into place so that the pressure within the bottle will not cause it to move. A metallic or other type of hood adds to the physical presentation of the product.

Ordinary bottle caps lined with cork or plastic will protect a mead, including a sparkling mead, as well as a cork does. They may not be as romantic as corks, but they are certainly practical.

## Carbonation

A sparkling alcoholic beverage usually has about five atmospheres (60 pounds) of pressure, many times the pressure of a can of beer or soda water. There are laboratory gadgets for measuring the pressure in a sparkling beverage, but they are expensive and cumbersome. The judge must make a visual assessment, based on experience, to determine if the pressure of a sparkling mead is adequate.

Figure 26. Baked goods at a show.

# Chapter 13.
# Baked Goods and Candy

It is our opinion that baked goods and candy entered in a honey show should be made using only honey as a sweetener. At some honey shows, as little as 25 percent of the sweetener is honey. This is an area in which the rules must be carefully studied by those who enter. Most recipes calling for maple syrup or sugar can be converted to honey as the sweetener. It is a challenge for devoted cooks to find the recipes in which honey blends the best.

## Rules

The most important consideration in a honey baked goods and candy class is the quantity of honey that should be used. Several other considerations are discussed below.

*Recipe* — Entries should be accompanied by a copy of the recipe, preferably on a 3- by 5-inch card. The recipe should either be printed or typed with no name or address. Handwriting, while it may be attractive, should not be used because it is not always legible. The recipe should be attached to the entry in a clear, easily opened plastic envelope. The judge reads the recipe, taking note of the sweetener and how it is used. If it is the policy of the group sponsoring the show to publish the recipes, or selected recipes, this should be stated in the rules.

*Presentation* — None of the entries should be sliced or cut. All food products should be presented in a container or on a plate that is sufficiently large and sturdy. The physical appearance of the plate or container is important and can enhance the attractiveness of the product. The entries should be covered with a thin, clear plastic wrap. When the entry consists of several pieces (such as cookies), it should be appropriately arranged. The judge needs paper plates, napkins, a knife and fork, water to drink and clear the palate, and a waste basket to dispose of the excess. These should be supplied by the show superintendent, but if the judge is responsible for providing them it should be made clear in the rules.

*Quantity of the entry* —The quantity of the product required varies with each show. As a display, it is nice to have a good showing of the product. On the other hand, food supplies are expensive. A cake, for example, after being exhibited for several days, is usually discarded. The judge needs only a mouthful of food for tasting. Even if three judges are present, one muffin, cookie, or roll is enough for the three. The quantity of the product to be displayed should be discussed by the show committee and is not the concern of the judge.

## Discussion of the judging card (baked goods)

Judging cards for baked goods and candy classes vary greatly, but cards from other food shows (with an emphasis on fruits, nuts, or other food products) may sometimes be used.

## Lightness

Lightness does not refer to the color but the consistency of the product. Breads should be substantial but not heavy. They should be medium to fine grained with no air bubbles. Cakes, depending on the kind, should be light and have a good volume for the size. Cookies may be light or substantial. Pies are rarely light, except for chiffon. The cook must be aware of what the consumer expects in each product.

## Texture, grain, moisture, uniformity of color

The moisture level, grain, and color should be uniform throughout the product. In breads, the crust should be a golden brown and the interior should not have air bubbles. (*Note:* A crack on the top of a loaf of bread is acceptable, but placing an inverted pan of the same size over the bread during the first 20 minutes of cooking will usually prevent cracking.) The texture should be fine in cakes and more coarse in cookies and breads.

In all products the color should be uniform. A special advantage of honey is that it usually browns evenly with an attractive golden hue or color.

### General appearance

Uniformity is important. All products may lose points if they are burned or too dark, have run-over edges, or are dry, tough, or soggy. They must have an even surface that is not cracked or bubbled. Frostings should not be runny or sugary.

A judge opens all products to taste and check the above qualities. Products whose seals make opening difficult waste the judge's time.

### Flavor

All products should have a distinct and appealing flavor. Proper blending is often the key.

### Discussion of the judging card (candy)

The same card may be used for baked goods and candy because some of the considerations overlap.

### General appearance

The consistency of a product is very important and perhaps the most difficult quality to satisfy. The candy must be appropriate to its type: chewy, hard, soft, etc. The length of the cooking time is of utmost importance. A candy thermometer is a "must." Dipped candies must have a uniform exterior appearance.

### Flavor

A flavor appropriate to the product is expected.

### Texture

Candy must not be grainy or sugary, but well-blended and uniform.

### Handling quality in serving

A candy must not be too sticky to handle since it is most often consumed by hand.

# Chapter 14. Governments and the Grading of Honey and Beeswax

Only a few states have their own grading systems for honey (and other agricultural products). Most follow federal guidelines. In Europe, the *Codex Alimentarius* is widely used. It makes use of diastase and hydroxymethylfurfural levels, which are not true indictors of honey quality and have never been used in this country by beekeepers or honey buyers. Diastase is a heat-sensitive enzyme that is not present in equal quantities in all honeys. Hydroxymethylfurfural is derived from sucrose and is also thought to be an indication of the overheating of honey, but is not uniformly so.

### The U.S. Department of Agriculture's grading system

It is difficult to respect the system that the Department of Agriculture uses to grade agricultural products because of the variety of terms used. For example, beef is graded Prime, Choice, and Good, while eggs are graded AA and A. Comb honey is graded as U.S. Fancy, U.S. No. 1, No. 2, and No. 3. The grades for liquid honey are A, B, C, and D, although at one time the term U.S. Fancy could be used for extracted (liquid) honey. These are only a few of the variations

*Figure 27. Pfund grader.*

*Figure 28. USDA color comparator.*

and this mixture of words, letters, and numbers is obviously misleading to many people.

## Grades for liquid honey

The grades used for extracted (liquid) honey are published under the title United States Standards for Grades of Extracted Honey, effective May 23, 1985. This is the fifth issue of the grades for extracted honey since grades were first proposed. The 11-page brochure containing the grades is available from the Processed Products Branch, Fruit and Vegetable Division, Agricultural Marketing Service, U.S. Department of Agriculture, Washington, D. C. 20250. These were published in the Federal Register on April 23, 1985 (50 F. R. 15861), superseding grades that had been in effect since April 16, 1951. The earlier standards had been published in the Federal Register of March 16, 1951 (16 F.R. 2463), recodified on December 9, 1953 (18 F.R. 8005), and amended (22 F.R. 3535) to be effective July 1, 1957.

## Equipment for grading honey

The Pfund grader was designed by the U.S. Department of Agriculture's Office of Bee Culture Investigations in 1925. It is named after Dr. A. H. Pfund, a physicist and specialist in colorimetry at Johns Hopkins University. Pfund and several members of the Bee Culture Laboratory, especially Dr. E. L. Sechrist, were instrumental in its design.

In 1927, the grader was made the official instrument for the color grading of honey and continued to be so used until it was replaced by the U.S. Department of Agriculture's color comparator in 1951 (see below). Despite this official change in status, the Pfund grader has remained the standard for grading honey in the beekeeping industry because of its accuracy. It is still cited in the latest (1985) U.S. Standards for Extracted Honey, leading one to question which grader is more important, even to the U.S. Department of Agriculture.

The Pfund grader consists of a colored glass wedge and a glass trough in which one places slightly over an ounce of the honey to be graded. The wedge of honey is mounted above the colored glass wedge on a movable frame. The movable frame is ratcheted in one direction or the other so that the colored wedge and the wedge of honey may be viewed in opposition to each other through a narrow slit on the face of the grader. When their colors match, a number is read from a permanently attached scale near the top of the grader. The color value ranges from 0 (water white) to 140 (coal black).

The Pfund grader is designed to be a precise instrument, and with a small amount of experience one may obtain remarkably uniform readings from one reading to the next on the same instrument. It is especially useful in making honey blends. There have been complaints that the instruments are not uniform from one machine to the next. The Pfund grader has several disadvantages: it is expensive; the colored glass wedge may fade with time; each grader should be recalibrated at least every ten years; a fairly large amount of honey, an ounce or more, is needed to determine the color grade; the honey must be liquefied before it is graded; the grader must be cleaned between samples.

The original Pfund grader had five standard grades, as indicated in the table below. However, under pressure from western beekeepers who produced lighter honey, the grades of extra white and extra light amber were added. The official grades are listed in the table below, whether one is using the Pfund grader or the U.S. Department of Agriculture color comparator.

## Pfund Color Grades for Honey

| Color Grade Value | Pfund Grade |
| --- | --- |
| water white | 8 or less |
| extra white | 9-17 |
| white | 18-34 |
| extra light amber | 35-50 |
| light amber | 51-85 |
| amber | 86-114 |
| dark | over 114 |

The history of the Pfund grader is discussed in the following paper: Fell, R. D. 1978. The color grading of honey. *American Bee Journal* 118: 782-783, 789.

## The U.S. Department of Agriculture color comparator

The color comparator was developed by the U.S. Department of Agriculture in 1951. It was stated by researchers in this agency at the time that the Pfund grader was not practical for field use (which is true) and that a simpler grader was needed. Before the comparator was released, several laboratories and companies that owned and used Pfund graders were given coded samples of honey by this research team and asked to grade them on their grader. The results were widely different depending on the age of the grader's color wedge. It was demonstrated clearly that the color wedges on the Pfund grader fade in time and that each grader must be recalibrated at least every ten years. The developers of the comparator felt that this was a serious fault and that a comparator with a longer life was needed. History has shown that the life of the U.S. Department of Agriculture's comparator is even shorter because the fluids evaporate and the color bars also fade. The comparator is available, but little used today. The Pfund grader remains the most widely used instrument for grading honey color. It is especially popular with the larger honey packers. The original paper describing the color comparator is: Brice, B. A., A. Turner Jr., J. W. White Jr., F. L. Southerland, L. S. Fenn, and E. P. Bostwick. 1951. Permanent glass color standards for extracted honey. *Gleanings in Bee Culture* 79: 410-412.

## Lovibond color grader

The Lovibond color grader for honey is sold by the Tintometer Company (Busch Corporate Center, 309A McLaws Circle, Williamsburg, VA 23185). It is based on calorimetric techniques designed by Dr. Lovibond over 100 years ago in Germany. While it is reasonably accurate, it has never gained wide acceptance in this country. Its chief virtue is that it is much cheaper than any other grader.

## Grades for comb honey

The grades for comb honey are found in a nine page brochure entitled "United States Standards for Grades of Comb Honey Effective May 24, 1967." These are available from the U. S. Department of Agriculture at the address listed in "Grades for Liquid Honey."

## Grading beeswax

There are no official (government) grades for beeswax. The American Wax Importer's and Refiner's Association Inc. has published a paper entitled "Specifications, genuine pure beeswax" that is reprinted by Coggshall and Morse (1984). While these specifications are reasonable, they are seldom mentioned and little

*Figure 29. Bees constructing new wax comb.*

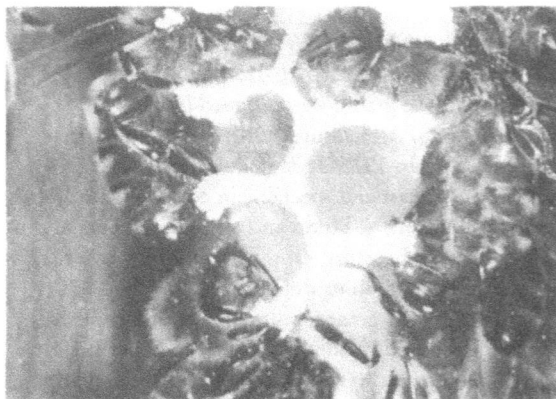

used. The color of the beeswax is especially important to buyers. Most beeswax buyers depend on their senses of odor and taste to test beeswax. Bleached beeswax is devoid of both, and those who sell beeswax for candle making, and especially to cosmetic firms, depend upon their reputations for repeat sales (Coggshall, W. L. and R. A. Morse. 1984. *Beeswax, Production, Harvesting, Processing and Products.* Wicwas Press, Cheshire, CT).

# Chapter 15. Addenda and Anecdotes

We have gathered below a few of the many notes that have been passed on to us by successful honey show exhibitors.

## A note on comb honey

Raymond Churchill of Watertown, N.Y. won several blue ribbons and silver bowls for his comb honey entries in Eastern Apicultural Society honey shows. Granted, he lived in an area known for its high-quality clover honey, but being a consistent winner requires more than good luck and a good location. Churchill was always willing to discuss comb honey production with anyone who is interested. He has written about his management scheme (Churchill, R. 1992. Shook swarm method of comb honey production. *American Bee Journal* 132: 227-229).

Churchill's method is to shake the bees and the queen from a colony into a shallow super with new frames and foundation and add two comb honey supers. The supers and brood combs are given to another colony. This is done at the outset of the honey flow, not before. Several little considerations must be taken into account for the method to work. At any rate, the fact is that Churchill has been a great success in the comb honey arena, and his paper is well worth careful reading.

Churchill once told me a little trick thaty is not mentioned in his paper. In some years he would establish a single colony in an area a mile or so away from other colonies and use this to produce comb honey for shows. This colony would have less competition in the immediate area and might benefit as a result.

This can be especially important in years when the honey flow is poor and resources are limited.

## Another note on exhibiting comb honey

Eugene Killion of Illinois is another beekeeper who has won multiple silver bowls and blue ribbons, especially at the National Honey Show. He has written a book on comb honey production (*Honey in the Comb.* 1981. Dadant and Sons, Hamilton, Illinois. 148 pages). While most of his book is concerned with production techniques, he devotes an eight-page chapter to preparing comb honey for shows. Chunk honey packs are also discussed in detail. The book is very well illustrated. Cleanliness and the physical appearance of an entry are emphasized. A facsimile miniature blue ribbon that states, "1st Prize, National Honey Show," is illustrated and shown affixed to a section that is being offered for sale. It is a nice addition to a package and a good sales promoter. Killion's book is a fine addition to a beekeeper's library.

## A note on clarifying liquid honey

The late Floyd Sandt of Pennsylvania was a beekeeper and honey packer who won several blue ribbons at some of the early Eastern Apicultural Society honey shows. We once asked him how he prepared his liquid honey for shows. He replied that he packed his honey for retail sale from tall tanks that held approximately one ton of honey each. Two or three weeks before a show he would fill one of these tanks. The honey was heated to about 140 degrees F in order to pasteurize it. The tank of honey was allowed to cool slowly and was left untouched for about two weeks. At that point the honey was bottled. Three jars were selected for exhibiting when the tank was half empty. Mr. Sandt allowed natural settling to clarify his honey. In this way, any air bubbles and debris that were present settled slowly to the top of the tank. His show samples always were of high quality.

One does not need a one-ton tank to settle and clarify honey properly; a smaller tank will work just as well. Time and temperature are the important considerations. Air bubbles and debris in cool honey take longer to settle to the top than those in warm honey. Of course, honey that is kept warm for too long will darken and be damaged.

# Index

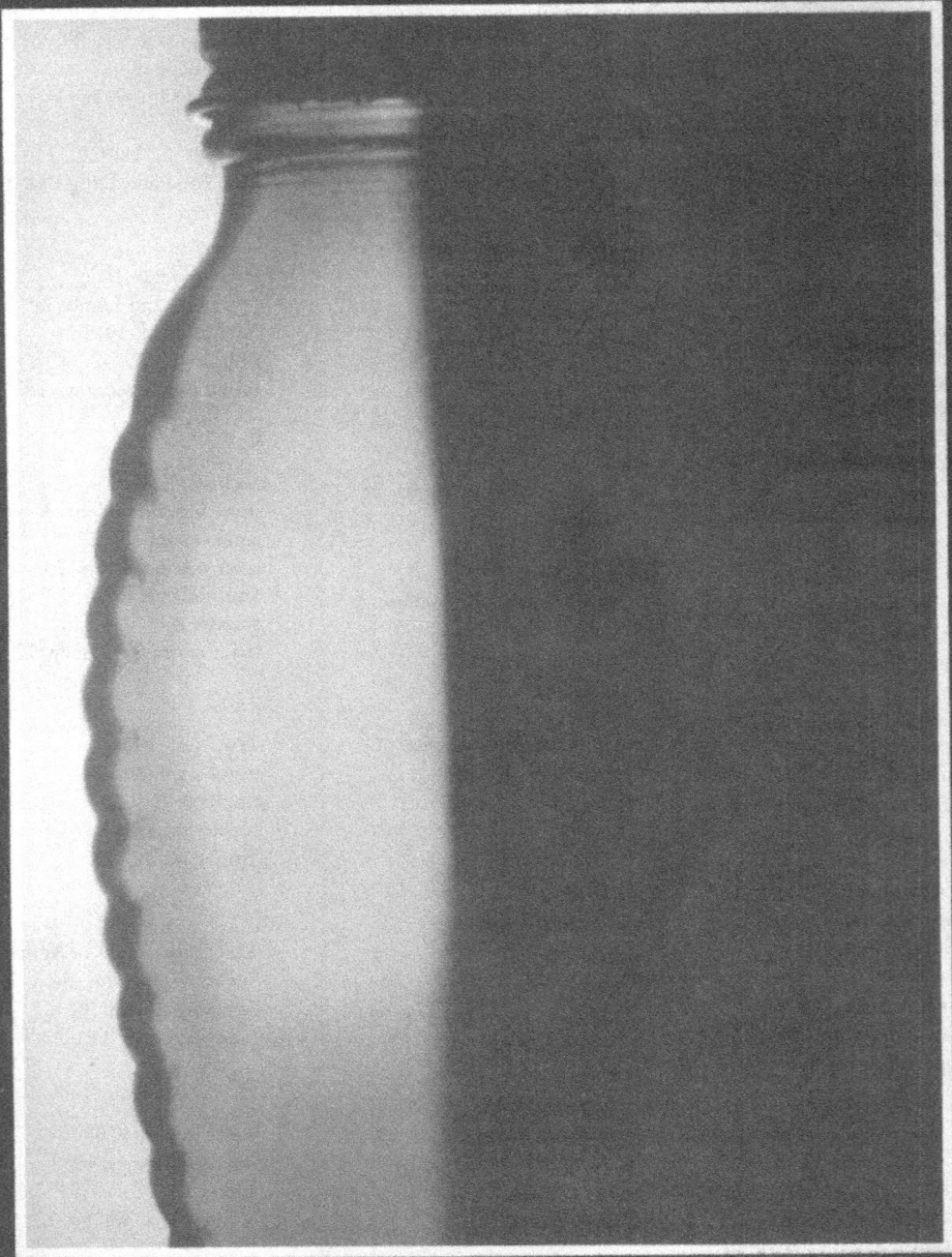

Viewing a jar of honey through polarized film (right side of photo) shows granulated sugar crystals. While a natural process, crystallization reduces both honey clarity and product shelf life.

ISBN 1-878075-07-1 ■ Wicwas Press, LLC, P.O. Box 817, Cheshire CT 06410-0817

www.ingramcontent.com/pod-product-compliance
Lightning Source LLC
Chambersburg PA
CBHW081142090426
42736CB00018B/3446